CHILDREN'S CHURCH:

Turning Your

CIRCUS

into a

SERVICE

DICK GRUBER

Gospel Publishing House
Springfield, Missouri
02-0680

To Darlene, my wife and friend

© 1992 by Gospel Publishing House, Springfield, Missouri
65802-1894. All rights reserved. No part of this book may be
reproduced, stored in a retrieval system, or transmitted in any form
or by any means—electronic, mechanical, photocopy, recording, or
otherwise—without prior written permission of the copyright
owner, except brief quotations used in connection with reviews in
magazines or newspapers.

Library of Congress Catalog Card Number 92–72192

International Standard Book Number 0–88243–680–5

Printed in the United States of America

★ ★

CONTENTS

OUR MINISTRY BEGINS

My fiancée, Darlene, and I followed the children down the rusty bus steps, across the parking lot, and into the church. For several weeks we had been helping as song leaders on a church bus. (At the time we didn't know this was called ministry. We were just wanting to serve God any way we could.) But this Sunday we were headed to the sanctuary.

It seemed an ordinary enough morning that Sunday in the spring of 1975. People attended Sunday school, walked their dogs, slept in, yelled at their children. The sky was overcast and the snow melted enough to birth hopes of the coming green. But in looking back I see the significance that Sunday played in the revelation of God's plan for me, my wife to be, and the children we would have at home and church.

The children pushed their way up the stairs, through the doors, and into the sanctuary. Seating was found amidst giggles, wonderment, and a few choruses being played on the grand piano. Mrs. Walker stood and opened in prayer. That prayer opened the service, but more than that it introduced me to children's church.

Oh, I had visited once before. It was an accident really.

Or perhaps it was one of those amusing, amazing times when God steps into the life of one of His children. My first Sunday at Glad Tidings had found me arriving early, finding a seat in the balcony, and witnessing my first children's church service. I was amazed as children enjoyed worship, preaching of the Word at their own level, and a time of prayer. *This is for me!* I had decided that day. When the time was right and the opportunity offered, I became an official helper.

However, that first day as a children's church helper was uneventful. I don't remember the message preached or the songs sung. I do recall the presence of God and the joy of being part of an important ministry in the church. God, in His infinite wisdom, had placed me in a children's church.

For almost a year and a half Darlene and I served in that children's church. Eventually the leader even let us minister up front. During that year we were married, had our first child, and learned how to operate a puppet. (God is so good.)

Since that rather ordinary beginning, we have served in four churches in three states. Each church has introduced us to new opportunities, traditions, and friends. Each state has witnessed the birth of another Gruber child. (We are not planning on another move.)

The children's churches that Darlene and I have served in over the years have varied in numbers and styles: In one church we had a group of 12. In another we had a group ranging from 70 to 120, depending on what kind of Sunday it was and whether or not my ushers counted the puppets. The largest church averaged 150 to 175, with a high attendance of 317 one Easter Sunday morning.

We have worked with a variety of ages as well as numbers. In one setting, children 4 to 11 years old were encouraged to attend. Another saw kindergarten through 6th grade. Now we serve the 4th, 5th, and 6th graders.

I have written this brief history of our children's church ministry so that you might know I am one like you. A formal education is mine, but a far deeper education has been wrought as I have cried with, prayed for, and ministered to His little children.

Names such as Dan Hines, Elaine Walker, Dan Rector, Bob Hahn, Jim Wideman, and George Edgerly will forever be locked in my memory as contributors to the Dick Gruber that writes this book.

More than to the support of good friends and mentors, I must give credit to the children: the children of Eden Prairie and Farmington, Minnesota; of Salem, Oregon, and of Springfield, Missouri; and, of course, the children who live in my home, teaching me daily what a good children's church leader should be and how he should live. Sarah, Aaron, Rachel, and Timothy have defined and redefined my understanding of worship, attention span, and ministry.

Finally, I salute my wife, Darlene. Her support and editorial skills have contributed greatly to the finished product.

I am a children's church leader sharing with children's church leaders. My prayer is that you will enjoy and benefit from this work.

1

★ ★

FROM A CIRCUS TO A SERVICE

CIRCUS vs. SERVICE

CIRCUS	SERVICE
. . . noisy	. . . calm, cool, collected
. . . confusion	. . . everything in order
. . . audience/performer	. . . total group participation
. . . no theme	. . . central theme
. . . fun, temporal	. . . excitement, eternal joy
. . . ringmaster	. . . pastor
. . . popcorn, candy	. . . God's Word
. . . performance acts	. . . music, offering, specials

There are basic rules that we all live by. They begin with simple commands such as "No!" or "Don't lick the dog!" The Christian lives by the Ten Commandments. Striving to live the fruit of the Spirit, each one of us has a desire to be more like Jesus. Each one of us wants to do what is pleasing in God's sight.

Children's church, a circus or a service? That is the question. What are you running each Sunday morning?

Too often children participate week after week, year after year, in a three-ring attempt at church. Eventually they are promoted out of the children's department and are faced with the stark reality that the adults just don't have puppets and prizes each week. Such children often go through a kind of culture shock when introduced to adult worship and cease participating in the service altogether.

The children's church should be planned with this worthy goal in mind: Everything demonstrated and sung and spoken and prayed should be done for the glory of God. All elements of the program should be working toward that day when the child graduates into sixty or seventy years of adult worship.

The children's church should be just what the name implies: a training ground for the saints of God who, because of age, have been called children.

For that reason, the children's church worship experience should encourage children to be the Church. Each child can be encouraged to participate. The Church, the body of Christ, in its preadolescent form must be instructed, inspired, and instilled with militant Christlikeness.

In simpler terms, it is time to get children off the quiet seats and into the ministry. "Train up a child in the way he should go . . ." This brings dreams of well-behaved little ones happily obeying every rule, wearing miniversions of ministerial-type attire and being able to quote vast passages of Scripture. To realize the fruit of this proverb, however, requires daring discipleship. It calls for careful cultivation of Christlikeness in children who may not wear designer clothing. The teacher must learn to let the children come to Jesus in children's church and upon arriving, teach each other.

Now picture the main church service for adults. There sits an incredible pool of talent which may never rise beyond spiritual bench warming. These believers were taught in Sunday school and children's churches of yesteryear to sit quietly and listen to the lesson. They were never allowed to hold the object of the object lesson, tell the story, or lead the chorus.

Their teachers were considered model in every way. Each class was a case study in the art of discipline. Yet these students grew into a lethargic adulthood. Now they sit in serene Sunday repose week after dreary week. These adults are doing what they were compelled to do as children. They have been trained in the way they should not go, and now they are old and will not depart from it.

Let me encourage you to use children in ministry. Let the children's church be a training ground for the younger Church of today. Make the service answer the simple longing in every saint that is satisfied only in serving. Provide each child with opportunities to minister according to his ability.

There are many variations to what is called a children's church. Some have successfully utilized the extended session. In this approach, the children remain with their particular age groupings the entire Sunday morning. The children's church time may include a staff change and some type of song service and methodology that differs from the Sunday school. However, the extended session usually will emphasize the same theme throughout the church time as was presented during the Sunday school hour.

For the younger elementary and preschool child, this approach is fabulous. These children need the continuity of theme for the entire Sunday experience. They must be instructed through a hands-on environment that cries, "Touch and feel and discover the reality of a living God."

On the other hand, the circus promotes an audience-performer atmosphere. Hold onto your seats while the juggling puppets perform Handel's *Messiah*. I have witnessed this praise-a-matic pandemonium hour. It occurs with disturbing frequency. The hour and a half to two

11

The praise-a-matic pandemonium hour

hours seem to follow no theme other than that of Bible babysitting made difficult. Snacks, games, and special requests fill a time slot in which no sane adult wants to serve.

The resulting confusion, dissatisfaction, and depression among the workers cause a high burnout rate. It is no wonder that people in such a church feel that children's church is a time of babysitting.

In this book we will not study these types of programs. Instead, emphasis will be placed on the superchurch concept which has become so prominent across this country. However, I will not impose sample schedules on you. Your facilities, pastor, and patience have already determined the appropriate course. Rather, I will present the ideal to strive for in your children's church.

The ideal is a church service; every service challenges service. The children we serve are saints; every saint is a participant. They are the body of Christ; everybody should be active in the Body.

So from this book, apply what will work in your setting. Underline and quote to your pastor or board those portions that may affect your future positively. Dissect and distribute the parts that will turn your children's church into a real worship experience for the children. Pray through the portions that demand a transformation of the children's church. Then make it into a training ground that provides meaningful transition into adult and family worship.

In short, close down the greatest show on earth, pack away the fixings of the circus, and begin to experience the freedom of a service.

If that last statement coincides with your sense of right, then keep reading. Don't put this down until you have devoured every dogmatic delicacy within its pages. If it makes you mad, give it a chance. It may strike that chord of deeper truth which you have been searching for in your weekly struggle.

You can have a children's church. The methodology can continue to be colorful and interesting. There is still a place for your puppets and prizes; the gospel must be preached to the children in an exciting manner. But in the midst of your Sunday morning you can put the circus days behind you. You can become the leader of a service.

2

★ ★

LEADERSHIP: FINDING THE RIGHT STYLE

We have already mentioned some types of children's church programs. The type of program, philosophy of pastor and board, and other uncontrollable variables will determine the style of leadership you may use.

At times, a person is thrust into a particular leadership style until relief comes. When it does, then the leader has opportunity to investigate and experiment with other ways to lead the children in worship. The form relief assumes is in the faithful assistance of other saints. These people may not have doctorates in children's ministries, but their zeal, teachable attitude, and faithfulness provide the help and time for reflection.

I personally have used three distinct leadership styles. When I became a children's church helper, I served on a team with other volunteers. Then, in my first years as a children's pastor, I did almost everything myself. Eventually I began utilizing and training laypeople to do the work of the ministry. Now I find myself serving as a volunteer with other volunteers assisting me. (My current style closely resembles a combination of the second and third models discussed in the following pages.)

Each of the three styles presented will work in its own time and place. Take a look at them as they are described in the following pages. Examine your leadership style in light of them and then take inventory. Evaluate the effectiveness of your own style. You may want to adapt it or change it altogether. The wise leader continues to grow and learn. I have, and you can too.

HARVEY HOG SUNDAY MORNING SIDESHOW

Early in my career as a children's pastor, I produced and starred in the "Harvey Hog Sunday Morning Sideshow." Being young and unused to working with others, I found the Harvey Hog method was the easiest way to run the service.

At the time, I had not yet come to understand Ephesians 4:11 and 12. The Scripture plainly teaches that a teacher, pastor, or children's church leader has one major task: to prepare the saints for works of ministry. A leader who hogs the pulpit, never allowing adults or children to assist, has failed in the prime directive of Ephesians 4.

Take a look at the characteristics of the Harvey Hog Sunday Morning Sideshow. The first requirement is that Harvey do it all.

Harvey arrives at church on a typical Sunday morning with an arsenal of the latest methods. His arsenal includes puppets, prizes, an electronic keyboard (with sixty-six keys and over three thousand possible sampled sounds), a puppet stage, a flannel board, an overhead projector, and a diaper bag containing anything he might need should the pastor get blessed and preach till sundown. Harvey may even have a Bible.

This leader believes in the old adage, If you want something done right, you better do it yourself, bless God!

Harvey Hog equips himself with an arsenal of latest methods.

He staggers his way toward the children's church room opening his own doors. After all, if someone else held them open they might release one too soon. The result would be catastrophic.

Harvey Hog sets up the children's church equipment behind closed doors. This is a top secret project; the eyes of others may spoil the effect of a special lesson he has planned for the children.

When the moment of truth arrives, Harvey heartily welcomes the children to church. He seats the children and calls them to order. Any stray adults that have entered the room stand at the back or exit. Harvey opens the service in prayer.

The Harvey Hog Sunday Morning Sideshow is only as well-organized as the one in charge. In my case, this was a fine-tuned farce. Once in a while I even allowed my wife to take part. When I did, occasionally she knew her assignment three or four days early; at other times she knew it three or four minutes before children's church began.

If the leader in such a service is disorganized, the children will generally plan the service for him. Children are very creative when it comes to planning service or class time for the disorganized teacher. The flaw in allowing this to continue is the subject matter and methodology employed. The little darlings could be teaching something you do not want people to learn, examples being primitive methods of wallpaper removal, stacking metal folding chairs, or puppet decapitation.

All kidding aside, the Harvey Hog service will maintain a consistent quality. I have never known a Harvey Hog who was not conscientiously doing his best. At the worst, he is an untrained, misguided, boring individual. In his most advanced state, this leader can do wonders with a group of children.

I have several friends who easily fit in this category.

They have been "successful" children's church leaders for many years. Congregational attitudes being what they are, these leaders have done an admirable job.

If you fit into this category, I encourage you to closely examine the next two and see how you might begin to involve others.

What do we know about the Harvey Hog Sunday Morning Sideshow? We know that it has these main characteristics:

1. Everything done by one person (paid or not)

2. No help, adult or children, allowed

3. Possibly well-organized (dependent on his ability)

4. Consistent quality (good, bad, or boring)

ALPHA AND OMEGA AMATEUR HOUR

A symphony of Christian ability, the Alpha and Omega Amateur Hour is a swing of the proverbial pendulum. Where Harvey has a monopoly on the ministry, Alpha and Omegas strive to produce a community effort. There is no "professional" figure pulling the strings here. There is no ambitious general pushing his way to the top.

Here you find many members with a singular purpose. This is a group of cooperative individuals who have a deep concern for the spiritual growth and well-being of the children. It was in such a group, in Eden Prairie, Minnesota, that I discovered much of the methodology that I presently use. The memories of those days are both joy-filled and scary.

A constant in every Alpha and Omega Amateur Hour is a deep commitment of the team members. The group generally consists of intelligent, caring individuals who have no great need for pastoral back-patting. They live Colossians 3:23, "Whatever you do, work at it with all your heart, as working for the Lord, not for men." In their veins runs the lifeblood of faithfulness, generosity, sincerity. These are the kind of people that support the church with their time, talents, and finances.

A typical Sunday morning will find the Alpha and Omega Amateurs hauling wheelbarrow loads of equipment into the church. They stay up most Saturday nights creating new forms of subatomic puppetry and adventures of the potato people. They creatively use the normal of every day to demonstrate the supernatural of eternity.

The Alpha and Omega crowd is prone to prayer. They recognize the need for total dependence on the Holy Spirit's guidance. There is no professional directing these saints. Theirs is a children's church guided by a strong love for the children and a unity of spirit. In most cases, these people willingly submit to whatever leadership the church provides. The Alpha and Omega team looks forward to the day when they can turn the children's church over to a genuine children's pastor. They are definitely a team committed to prayer (and people of prayer tend to be selfless).

Variety is the spice of children's church. An Alpha and Omega team provides much variety in both methodology and ability. The children will see many faces. This can be wonderful in a team that is well-organized and of one mind. On the other hand, a loosely run team, in spite of good intent, can bore, frustrate, or even confuse the children.

I have painted a very positive picture of the Alpha and Omega Amateur Hour. This is a result of my own posi-

The Alpha and Omega crowd is deeply committed.

tive experience in such groups. At the same time, I offer some cautions: Should the team lack in organization, prayer, or team spirit, disaster can prevail. The Alpha and Omega Amateur Hour can very well be the circus we are wanting to avoid. A strong, spiritual master of ceremonies who lovingly allows all team members to express their gifts is the key to a successful team.

The church that cannot afford a children's pastor should actively recruit and train such a team as I have described. Monthly training and planning times must be provided.

Let us review the basic characteristics of the Alpha and Omega Amateur Hour.

1. Many members with a singular purpose

2. Commitment to the Word, the church, and the children

3. People of prayer

4. A variety of faces and methodology

5. Depends on a competent leader to work well

FLASH AND THE FIVE REFLECTIONS

He steps to the microphone as a hush of expectancy sweeps over the children. In his hands he holds a Bible and a rubber chicken. Standing in Goliath proportion to those first graders in the front row, Flash opens the service in prayer. What follows is a finely tuned team of laypeople led through the service by this trainer of others.

Each moves with purpose; each ministers at the appointed time, as Flash ties the segments of the service to a central theme. At the conclusion, he leads in prayer and the children go out. They have encountered the living God as presented by Flash and the Five Reflections.

The most significant characteristic of this team is found in the leader. I have seen Flash in the eyes of a fifty-year-old woman as well as those of a twenty-four-year-old Bible college graduate. Flash is a person on whom the hand of God rests. He is sometimes paid for a job titled "children's pastor," a task he would gladly take on without pay. This laborer is worthy of his hire, yet would never require reimbursement for God's work.

Yes, my friend, Flash is the professional children's worker in calling, if not by title. He lives his life satisfied to be serving the most important age group in the world: children. Flash is confident in his calling. So much so that when well-meaning relatives ask, "Are you going to be a real pastor someday?" He suppresses the urge to say, "What do you mean, you ignorant buffoon? I am a real pastor." How does Flash respond? A smile, a song, a buzz handshake, and a statement something like this: "I thought I would just continue doing what Jesus would do. He would give His life for the children. Wouldn't you?" Flash finds this response to be effective.

Flash and the Five Reflections are the ultimate in Christian discipleship training. Pastor Flash recruits, trains, and inspires his children's church staff. He is an Ephesians 4:11 and 12 kind of guy, this servant of the saints who knows the value of allowing the laypeople to find a fulfilling place of ministry.

He knows that most of the lessons taught would be more professional, more pizzazz-filled, if he did them himself. But Flash is preparing the saints. He has discovered that a little trust in them will pay long-range dividends.

This team generally inspires an atmosphere of orderliness. It is a classic case of single-mindedness. Flash considers his team to be extensions of himself. They follow as he lovingly leads children to Christ. With numerous assistants, a variety of methodology, and the rejection of mediocrity on his side, the service is presented. Flash moves through each Sunday morning with his team at his side demonstrating Christian unity and love. The children sense the oneness of purpose through the attitudes and actions of this team. The result is a group of children who enjoy the children's church and therefore cause little or no disruption.

In my travels, it has been a joy to step to the platform and minister in a church that has such a team. I seldom spend any time at all reminding children in such a church of my rules. They are accustomed to paying attention in a spiritually sound, understandable, quality service.

Let's look once again at the characteristics of Flash and the Five Reflections.

1. Pastor with disciples (that is, volunteers)

2. Ongoing discipleship training of volunteers and children

3. One mind with many extensions

4. Atmosphere of orderliness

I have pointed out three specific types of leadership that may run the average children's church service. The wonder of God's grace is that each of them, or variations of them, works!

Encounter the living God as presented by Flash!

However, it should be apparent to you by now that I favor a leadership style that reflects the Ephesians 4:11 and 12 approach: Such leadership, whether paid staff or volunteer, constantly recruits and trains others for works of ministry.

Let me encourage you to evaluate your leadership style: Is it as effective as it can be? What could be done to make it better? How could you reproduce your talent, your vision, in the largest number of people possible?

Remember always to follow the leading of the greatest leader, Jesus. He discipled others. Touching the children, he blessed them, setting an example for his staff and the future of the Church.

3

★ ★

FROM A BALANCING ACT TO A BALANCED SERVICE

In the summer of 1980 I was experiencing the circus phenomenon on a weekly basis. Every conference I attended until then focused on methodology. Some of the biggest names in children's ministry were proposing that each children's church hour be a razzle-dazzle variety show.

One such instructor taught, "Kids are trained by the television. The average child has the attention span of a walnut. You must change activity every three to five minutes or you will lose him."

When I arrived home from that meeting, I replanned my upcoming children's church service. I interpreted the instructor's directive literally as I changed from lesson to song to chalk drawing to puppet all morning long.

I had determined to become the best vaudeville-like variety man in the business. I studied clowning, juggling, puppetry, ventriloquism, chalk drawing, music, balloon tying, and about 852 other visual methods.

My services were full of action-packed stories, up-tempo music, and bodacious surprises. Hours were spent perfecting the latest gospel magic trick, lip-syncing to the newest children's album, and practicing favorite chalk pictures. The children of my church were receiving the best in gospel entertainment.

That was the problem! The children were being entertained—not ministered to, or ministering.

One Sunday afternoon, following a particularly painful morning full of children who were intent upon forcing me to redefine discipline, I announced to my wife that God had lifted His hand from our ministry to children. It was time to go and become what some people affectionately referred to as a "real pastor." Darlene simply looked at me and said, "Did you talk to Jesus about this?"

"Well, uh, not recently I haven't," was my reply.

She smiled and barked, "Then don't talk to me about it! I have to get lunch in the oven."

God is so good. He gave me an honest and caring wife who doesn't pull punches when I am acting stupid. With her compassionate reprimand in focus, I began to pray. I also began to evaluate exactly what I was doing each Sunday morning.

The schedule ran something like this: Children entered the room to the most up-to-date, up-tempo children's music I could blast through the sound system. I opened with prayer and a reminder of the rules. This was followed by action songs, slow songs, a quick offering, a puppet special, a Scripture picture, an object lesson, another puppet special, an illustrated Bible story, a costume presentation, an instrumental special, a cartoon talk, an illustrated sermon, a quick prayer, and more songs. This cluttered routine was kept in motion until the adults retrieved their children.

So what is wrong with that? Weren't the children receiving some wonderful entertainment and fine preaching? Yes, but they were not experiencing church.

My service was out of balance. Children need more than well-timed puppets, phenomenal object lessons, and cliff-hanging stories. They need a service. I had been providing a circus, and they let me know of their disapproval through inappropriate behavior.

A service should be more than the pastor's preaching for an hour. Even if that preaching is delivered through a puppet and a chalk drawing. After prayer and introspection, I knew that my circus had to be transformed into a service. Some positive steps had to be taken.

Maintain balance for a vital and valid worship service.

My first step was to define in as few words as possible a purpose for meeting with the children. Why did we attend service? What did I expect to accomplish during the church time hour? What did I want the kids to know about the worship experience before they would be thrust into the adult worship mode?

Schedule of a Balanced Children's Church Service

OPEN: Rules*, Theme, Introduction, Prayer

WORSHIP

SONGS: "We Are Not Ashamed," "Cast Your Burden," (Praise Break), "I Been Praisin' Jesus," "Clapping Our Hands," "God is So Good," (Praise Break), "Come Bless the Lord"

PRAYER: For the sick and needy

GIVING

OFFERING: Lesson on missions, two girls singing

DRAMA: Four children presenting skit

PREACHING

SCRIPTURE PICTURE: John 3:30

BIBLE STORY: Emphasize principle theme

PUPPET SPECIAL: Theme related song

SERMON: Three theme enhancing illustrated points

PRAYER

ALTAR CALL: Prayer at the chair**

SPECIAL: If there is time, we will play a Bible quiz game of some kind or use a reinforcing object lesson

*See chapter 9. **See chapter 7.

A statement that I now deliver every week to the children came out of this time of evaluation: "We come together in this place to meet with each other and to meet with God."

This is what the adults do when they attend church, the great difference being comprehension and maturity levels.

I have come to view children's church as the opportunity for an authentic worship experience, which can prepare the child for meaningful transition into adult worship. The children learn respect for church facilities, leaders, and each other in children's church. The children will be in children's church for three to six years; they will spend fifty or sixty years in adult worship.

The children's church service should be geared to the children's level. It should include all of the exciting methods that gain their interest, but without the loss of authenticity.

Before the child reaches the age of promotion into adult worship I want him to know and experience Jesus Christ. He should be an active member of the body of Christ both in giving of his resources and his talent. I want to encourage in him a willingness to receive from God through the preached Word. His developing a desire for and experience of prayer are also essential. And finally I try to cultivate in them an attitude of servanthood by having them participate in practical ministry to their peers.

If these objectives were to be met, I realized that including the basic ingredients of a church service—and in the right proportion—would need to be practiced every week. Those ingredients included worship, giving, preaching, and prayer. When maintained in balance, they will supplant the circus with a vital and valid worship service.

The days of my preservice circus were filled with great preaching but lacked the other three ingredients.

I thought I really knew how to minister to kids. But there was no balance. Where there is no balance, the children's church dies.

Once I brought my service into balance, discipline problems dissipated, enthusiasm increased, and God began to touch all of our lives. Adults that visit such a service never again ask, "Do you ever miss going to church?"

This balance has not been achieved at the expense of the children. The kids still enjoy the excitement of gathering with their peers. They have been awakened to the joy of meeting with Jesus. Creative methodology is still employed. The leader is not on the road to burnout.

Balance your children's church. As you digest the rest of this book, begin to apply this principle of balance and the practical ideas given for achieving it.

I have employed the balance concept in three different church settings. It has worked in each. Balance your service and you'll never again wonder, *Is this a circus or a service?*

4

★ ★

WORSHIP FROM THE HEART

I served in children's church for four years before I discovered the beginnings of worship with the kids. We had marvelous song services. No one could accuse us of dull, dreary song times. There were action choruses, dance numbers, and a much needed slow song to calm the kids down for the rest of the circus.

But Psalty, the singing songbook of Kids Praise fame once said, "You can sing songs till you're blue in the face, but if it doesn't come from the heart, it's not praise." Our blue-faced friend makes a good point. Many children's services never stretch beyond a campfire sing-along. Week after week, children sing songs, yet rarely worship.

Before we discovered worship, my services went like this: From the time children entered the room, the air was filled with a "joyful noise." The sound system blared bouncy chords of happiness as children ricocheted off the pews.

We opened the program with a shout, a quick prayer, and action songs till workers dropped. This was the way I was taught. "A couple of fast songs will get some of the bugs out." What nobody told me was it would also activate the adrenalin gland of every moderately hyperactive child in the room.

We were not really experiencing worship.

What is worship but the personal act of ascribing worth to our loving Heavenly Father? It is the orchestrated heart-cry of the church in love with its Redeemer. Worship starts in the heart and spreads to the life. It is the action of a life totally sold out to Jesus, the overflowing expression of gratitude for the opportunity to live for Him.

Worship is the seven-year-old girl with tearstained cheeks praying words not memorized, but authored by the Spirit. Worship is the ten-year-old boy helping an elderly neighbor shovel snow, not for money or even thanks, but for his first love, Jesus.

In my study, I have found no passage of Scripture commanding us to teach children to worship. Oh, there are times mentioned in the Bible when children were present during worship, but I find no specific command to teach them how to worship. We are, however, compelled by numerous exhortations to teach the children God's Word.

In Matthew 21 we find Jesus preaching, teaching, and healing people in the temple area. Children spontaneously worship the revealed Christ. The religious leaders of the day wanted these embarrassing little ones to keep quiet. They should be seen and not heard.

The Matthew 21 principle for children's church is this: teach the Word, experience the presence of the Christ of the Word, and children will naturally worship God. It is not hard to encourage worship when a child is healed while his friends pray. Worship is no difficulty when the Holy Spirit touches the hearts of children. The children of Matthew 21 had no charismatic cheerleader hyping them into a frenzy of happy hosannas.

Though humanity is fallen, childhood has at least a remnant of innocence. When this innocence is presented with the love of God, children raise their voices in perfect worship. Jesus quoted the Scripture when he said,

★ ★

MATTHEW 21 PRINCIPLE

If you . . . 1. Teach the Word

　　　　　2. Experience the presence of
　　　　　　　the Christ of the Word

Then . . . Children will naturally worship

★ ★

"Haven't you ever read this Scripture? 'You have trained children and babies to offer perfect praise'" (TEV). God has perfected praise in the hearts and lives of children. Their honest assessment of God's worth is like no other music on earth.

So the task of a children's church leader becomes one of cultivating the seeds of worship which lie in the fertile soil of children's hearts. You are a gatekeeper. Each Sunday Jesus gives you the opportunity to swing wide that gate and let the praise of children out.

One method of opening the gate in any size group is the praise break. We have commercial breaks, why not praise breaks? Look through the Bible and find specific forms of praise, for example, "Be still, and know that I am God" (Psalm 46:10); "Shout unto God with the voice of triumph" (Psalm 47:1, KJV); "My mouth will declare your praise" (Psalm 51:15).

I usually hold praise breaks between songs, announcing the Scripture verse I'm using. I may say something like this: "Let us be doers of the Word today. The Bible says, 'Shout unto God with a voice of triumph!' We are all going to do what God's Word says right now. We are going to have a praise break. For the next fifteen seconds everyone in this room is going to be a doer of God's Word. We are all going to shout to God in a triumphant voice. Now, I will time you so you won't have to watch your watch. For just fifteen seconds we will shout to God. Maybe you have never done this before. That's okay. Everyone will be shouting praise to God. So when I say go, we will all shout to God for fifteen seconds."

Can you shout to God in praise for fifteen seconds?

When you're introducing the praise-break concept into your children's church, it is smart to begin with short periods of time. Fifteen seconds is an ideal length the first couple of breaks you take. After that you may grow in fifteen- or thirty-second increments and go as long as you like.

At times we have used two verses of Scripture as praise-break guidelines. A common example is the combination of "Be still, and know that I am God" (Psalm 46:10) and "lift up holy hands" (1 Timothy 2:8). The children quietly reflect on the love of Jesus while lifting their hands to heaven.

This practice for adult worship (as well as heaven) has revolutionized my children's church. Peer pressure has been turned around. The children who once stood back and felt that loving Jesus in public was dumb or boring now willingly praise Him with heart and voice. It is the acceptable practice to praise our Savior. After a slower song I might say, "Let's just be still and know that He is God." We lift up holy hands and whisper His praise.

Worship is the key to success in the continuation of your children's service. When the kids feel His presence, circus lights fade and service life begins. When children enter into worship, discipline problems solve themselves as hearts become receptive to the living God.

What do I do for music now? When the children enter our children's church, soft, soothing praise music is playing. This could be live or taped. I prefer Praise Strings. (Some of my buddies call it the Gruber funeral music.) I want the children to know that our meeting place is set aside for happenings of holiness, so that when they walk through the door they're ready to participate. Mellow worship music will allow the children to calm their spirits before God and ready themselves for a real service.

Once the children are seated and the service is opened we do use some action choruses and fast songs. Review what is being used in the adult or youth worship services at your church. Try to use the same songs or type of songs. Someday these kids will be in the youth and adult services. They should be prepared to make an easy adjustment into the worship offered in those settings.

You do not have to be a musician to lead children in

worship. If your children's church lacks a regular piano or guitar player, prerecord what is needed. Use my favorite background group, "The Cassettes."

Songs from Psalty's "Kid's Praise" albums are wonderful for children's church. The children do enjoy lively music as well as slow songs. Make an effort to sing Scripture choruses as much as possible. A time or two we have inserted classic hymns in our worship time. The majestic delivery of doctrinal truths in the old hymns is needed once in a while.

Integrity Music has also come out with some fabulous taped music for children's worship. This creative original is very usable.

From the faster action-type choruses we move into some slow ones with mellow praise breaks. During these there might be time given for testimonies. We are proclaiming the worth of Father God through lifted hands, voices raised, and specific personal praises for His goodness to us.

Every week I tell the kids that we are in this place to meet with each other and to meet with God. This is the all-important purpose of any church service. We have fellowship with one another; this is a place of encouragement. We have fellowship with God; this is a place of refreshment.

I realize that you may not dare to step into a bold style of worship immediately. Because of your background or church you may choose to move more slowly in that direction, making small, conservative changes. That's all right. Just begin the action. God will faithfully bless your willingness to give worship more emphasis and freedom.

Once children have had opportunity to worship, a service follows. This is a time of serving one another. We will serve through giving, preaching, and prayer.

The ideal transition from worship to giving is a time

of prayer for special needs. Some days I have the children who need prayer stand at their seats. Friends are encouraged to gather around and pray for them. Other times children with special requests come to the front of the room. I ask all others to be prayer partners. These partners stand or kneel beside or behind their needy friends and pray. In worship we have given praise and love to God. Now, through prayer, we give support and love to each other.

Evaluate the worship in your children's church. The worship sets the tone of the service, determining its effectiveness. Without true worship, the children's church is reduced to a circus. The attitude of the leader, the music, the atmosphere, all must be undergirded with fervent prayer.

Hold fast to a high standard in your worship. Do all you can under the loving guidance of the Holy Spirit and then step into your worship time with confidence. Taste and see the goodness of the Lord.

5

★ ★

GIVING ALL TO JESUS

You know the story. Children's church starts and it is really going smooth when suddenly you realize that it is offering time. Where are the buckets? Frantically you search or send someone else to search while you stall for time. Fumbling and bumbling around, your workers keep coming up empty-handed. Finally you give up on them and say, "Today we will walk past my open Bible. Let's just drop our money on its India paper pages—and be thankful that I let you out of your seat for a few moments."

Someway, somehow, offering has lost its place of honor in the children's church. If not looked upon as a time filler or an unwanted interruption, it is reduced to competitive and questionable craziness.

Like the ticket salesmen for the circus, we grab the money as fast as we can before the kids can change their minds about staying for the rest of the show.

When we relegate giving to a secondary place in the children's church, children will learn that giving is unimportant. When we treat giving as an annoying interruption, we imply that God is imposing on us.

When offering time becomes nothing more than a competition for cash, children lose sight of joyous stewardship.

Please do not misunderstand me. An occasional contest can serve to increase excitement and incoming funds. But "Give and thou shalt beat the girls" should not be the battle cry of the weekly offering time.

God loves a cheerful giver! I stepped into one service just as the boys were singing, "The boys beat the girls, the boys beat the girls, / Hallelujah, praise the Lord. The boys beat the girls!" (to the tune of "Farmer in the Dell"). I can honestly say those boys were cheerful. They were cheerfully rubbing the girls' noses in their failure to produce a winning financial report. This kind of farce fits well in a circus. But it is hardly an appropriate action or attitude for a true worship service.

When my children's church does enter the arena of competition, it will be with soft steps and a godly concern. I want to see every child that makes an effort feel like a winner. The widow's mite is still worth far more than the braggart's bucks.

Each month we set a Sunday aside for missions education and giving. Motivational incentives are sometimes used. If a child participates with even a penny, he will be rewarded. I want every boy and girl to grow up loving missions and missionaries. Where their treasure is their hearts will be also.

One method of educating the children about missions focuses on the passport. Each child is encouraged to bring a wallet-sized school picture. This is attached to the inside cover of a mock passport.

Each Sunday for one month the child will have his passport stamped if he remembers to bring some money for the missionaries. (Again, even a penny counts.) Keep a jar of nickles on hand in case children who visit come without any offering. At the end of the month, collect the passports and display them on a bulletin board.

The prize? Satisfaction received when parents and friends recognize a job well done. Every child will feel the joy of being part of the bigger picture.

I am serious about giving. Each time the children pass the hat, bucket, or bag, they are being educated. Giving offerings is a beautiful expression of love to our wonderful Savior.

Take a moment each week to give scriptural instruction on the joy of giving. My helpers are exhorted to prepare a lesson each time they are to handle offering time. A story, object lesson, or costumed presentation is a part of our giving time each week. Tithes, offerings, and missions should all be covered.

Keep in mind that the concepts you consistently teach through actions and words today can become a blessing or curse on your church body ten years from now. The child that is trained in the joyful act of giving now may some year be the church member who supplies the finances for your new sound system in children's church.

Further, if we really believe that children are part of the body of Christ, then our giving times will provide opportunities for children to express their ministry gifts. In other words, don't let the buck stop here. Teach the children to give every resource to Jesus. Children must learn to give their time and talents as well as their money to the One who gave His life to remove their sin.

Encourage children to use talents in ministry to one another. A child may sing, play an instrument, draw a picture, or present a drama. What a fabulous place for children to experience the joy of service! Serve the Lord with gladness. You will be blessed as children receive ministry from peers and respond to God.

One Sunday a girl named Kari presented a song during the offering. She stood trembling at the front of the room. The background tape began to play and she opened her mouth in song. The melody was one about heaven and as her ten-year-old voice resounded, something wonderful happened. Everyone in the children's church suddenly felt as if Jesus were in the room. Some wept, others sat in silence. At the conclusion of her song, all of us prayed. Kari had, for a brief time, become the minister. God honored her preparation and my trust in her as a member of His Body.

Jim and his sister Allison sang a duet recently. The song was one of hope that blessed everybody in the room. What an honor to allow a brother and sister to develop their talents in service of our King!

Aaron played his trumpet on a Sunday near Christmas. Sure the tune he played isn't considered a great hymn of the church ("Up On The Housetop"), but he was using his talent for Jesus.

We have included children giving their talents in art, drama, reading, music, juggling, doll collecting, and model building. The intent behind this is to find out what a child can do and allow him to do it for the glory of God. If a boy learns to fly model rockets, then have him bring one to class. As he shows it, teach about rising above the sin of this world.

So, my friend, let the children's church become the church of children! Create a balance which includes giving. Children will realize that you are indeed a good shepherd.

Your willingness to prepare the young saints for works of ministry will pay off in adults who feel a call to active service for the King. Someday a Sunday school teacher or

Children can develop talents in service of our King!

missionary will stand and testify that he began ministering as a child—in a children's church. That is where he discovered the wonderful feeling of being used by God to touch others. Giving of himself in ministry became a habit that the turmoil of the teenage years couldn't break.

In the meantime, your youth pastor will be blessed as you promote a ready force of ministers into his department each year. And parents will be amazed as their children relate incidents week after week of God's power demonstrated in and through the ministry of their peers.

The greatest joy I have experienced in children's ministries has been in witnessing God's hand on the ministry of a particular child, to watch children grow in concern for the lost, and to see a tangible expression of that concern.

Each children's church leader must ask at one time or

another, *Am I raising an army of pew potatoes?*

Children who are told week after week to sit down and be quiet will eventually do just that. Then as adults they will quietly sit and do nothing for God, for this is what they learned in children's church. The pastor will ask for help: He will beg for teachers to assist in the Sunday school and children's church. But these children of God have been trained in the way they should not go and now they are old and won't depart from it.

Begin this week to train up the children in the way they really should go: Teach them to joyfully assist with songs or tell a story or help their neighbor. Train them in godly attitudes of service to others.

Who knows, five years from now you may have a full force of willing, well-trained helpers who first caught the vision for ministry in your own children's church. Consider the giving time as recruitment for the future of the church. Allow children, the church of today, to give of their finances, their talents, their lives. Let them come to Jesus in complete joy and service. Teach them how to be willing vessels of honor for God.

Your faithfulness in this aspect of children's church creates a wonderful readiness in boys' and girls' hearts. They have worshiped Jesus in song, testimony, group prayer, giving of tithes and offerings, and ministry to one another. They are now ready to receive from God's Word in your preaching time.

6

★ ★

GET THE MESSAGE, THEN THE PUPPET (MAYBE)

I f you are anything like me, preaching is one of your favorite activities. It rates right up there with snorkeling off Molikini, playing expensive keyboards, or eating chocolate peanut butter ice cream.

Preaching is about the most natural thing a Christian can do, next to breathing. Christ commanded every believer to "go into all the world and preach the Gospel to every creature."

What a grand privilege it is to share the good news of Jesus with others! This opportunity is enhanced when you realize that God has allowed you to preach to His most precious souls: children. You are preaching in the children's church to those who best represent Christ in this world. If you give a cool cup of water to one of these little ones, you have given it to Jesus.

Perhaps you do not feel much like a big-time preacher. The words seemed to come so easily to the likes of Paul, Apollos, Luther, or Wesley. But remind yourself that God has chosen the foolish things of man to confound the wise. Most of the great revivals of history were preached by ordinary people who had received an extraordinary anointing of the Holy Spirit.

God is looking for a willing servant. You have been chosen to preach a life-giving message. Perhaps you have felt as if you were an accident waiting to happen. You were recruited, stuck in a children's church room, and left on your own. Do not fear! God loves the children of your church so much that He appointed you as part of their special ministry team. You are perfect for the job. A great harvest of souls is waiting for your faithfulness.

The preaching time is that portion of the service when a message from God is transmitted to the child. But where do you get such a message?

I strongly believe that the whole message cannot be found in a curriculum of any kind. Do not misunderstand. There are many fine curriculums on the market today. Each year it seems yet another creative children's pastor floods the market with his version of the perfect children's service curriculum.

When choosing a curriculum, begin to think of it as it was intended to be used: a recipe card. You are the Master's chef. God has allowed you the freedom to add to, or take away from, the content of curriculum and no curses will come upon you. Gather the ingredients that will best convey the theme to your children and make it palatable to them.

Would you invite your friends over for Sunday dinner and feed them recipe cards? Of course not! Even as they would expect a prepared meal, so would the children you serve. A pastor would not last long at any church if he read or recited Charles Spurgeon sermons every week. People expect the pastor to deliver a fresh word from the Lord. Children expect and need a fresh message from God in your preaching time each week.

If you are in the process of choosing a curriculum, let me give this simple bit of advice: Look first to your own denomination. If your denomination publishes a children's church curriculum, then that is the best source for you. My reasoning is simple. A quality curriculum published by your denomination will be the only curriculum that teaches your doctrine the way you believe it. Look to your denominational publishing house before spending big bucks on independent curriculums. Chances are you will receive just as much or more content than that in some of the fancy full-color notebooks available on today's market.

The curriculum becomes a base for a message from God. You may consult many other curricular sources in the preparation of that message. But please do not read word for word what was written by some other hand for a widespread audience of believers.

I look to the curriculum for a basic theme. Then I pray for God's anointing. I pray that God will give me a message as I study that theme in the curriculum and in His Word, the Bible.

Each day you should set aside time to pray and meditate upon that which you will teach or preach next week. A little a day keeps the burnout away. The Saturday night special may work for you once in a while, but soon the children will know that you are not prepared. Discipline will break down and the circus will begin.

In the preaching portion of children's church there are three things I always want to have: Scripture verse, Bible story, and illustrated sermon. I may or may not add puppets, object lessons, chalk talks, costume characters, life application stories, or a host of other methods. Keep in mind that the message is more important than the method.

I first look to God for the message; then I look to what methods will best speak to the children. Remember to always use language and concepts that the youngest child present will understand. Do not speak down to the children; talk with them. Be normal. There is nothing worse in a child's eyes than an adult that suddenly takes on a phony personality when preaching to kids. Be yourself and use language that will be understood.

★ ★

3 PARTS TO PREACHING
1. Scripture Verse
2. Bible Story
3. Illustrated Sermon

★ ★

There have been Sundays when I have simply addressed the children with an open Bible. Other times I go nuts with zany methods that expand the message before their eyes.

Try as often as possible to use all of the senses in preaching. One leader I know baked fresh bread on a Sunday morning. The children smelled the message, saw it, touched it, tasted it, and finally heard it as the leader preached about Jesus, the Bread of Life. You can be sure the kids will remember that message. Every time one of them enters a bakery he will think, *Jesus is the Bread of Life.*

I do want the message to be exciting. Some lessons are exciting even when they are no fun. In November 1979, a nine-year-old girl and her mother from our church were killed in a tragic accident. Children's church the next day was no fun at all. We cried together. We prayed together. We asked and attempted to answer questions. This message was no fun. It was, however, exciting as the children and I felt the presence of Jesus in that children's church room.

Church is always exciting when Jesus arrives. There may come times when you must deal with tough subjects that are not fun or that do not lend themselves to fun methods. Do not shy away from them. Trust Jesus and preach with confidence.

Do all you can to involve the children in your message. There are extroverted kids that will volunteer to act out every Bible story. Give them the opportunity. But do not fail to recognize the quiet children as well. A quiet or shy child can hand out papers, hold the object of an object lesson, or keep score in a quizzing contest. Involvement rates right up there with repetition as a key factor in learning retention. A child who participates in a lesson will be more apt to remember and apply that lesson throughout the week. Children can teach and preach to other children. As part of the body of Christ, every boy and girl has some ministry waiting to be discovered. Look for ways to allow children to serve children during the preaching time. I have found that object lessons are good, short, entry-level lessons for interested ministry hopefuls.

What methods are acceptable? I do not know your church as you do. Look to the leadership of your local body for direction. In one congregation the use of clowning and magic is no big deal, while in another it can be offensive. If I discover a certain method offends, I work with the offended one or I cease using the method.

I personally have tried many different media and methods, including role play, drama, costumed characters, clowning, mime, drawing, chalk talks, puppetry, ventriloquism, juggling, storytelling, slides, overhead projector, audio and video tapes, shadow puppetry, music, fire, magic, object lessons, discussion, games,

Scripture pictures, breakfast cereal, puzzles, chalkboard, flannelgraph.

I get ideas at conventions, toy stores, grocery stores, television, and from my own children. God is the most creative force of the universe. His Spirit dwells in the life of every believer. Draw upon this heavenly reserve and present your message in a creative new way this week.

Once a quarter we have game show Sunday. The theme will generally revolve around the idea of choices in life. Every game that is used will incorporate the theme in some rememberable way.

We also like to invite a missionary on occasion to minister to the children. Kids need to see that missionaries are real people. They must be exposed personally to these men and women of God. It is through such encounters that God calls children to full-time Christian service.

I was told by a man once that he was "ready to preach, pray, sing, die, or testify at a moment's notice." Does that ring a bell? In the children's church you will have times that call upon your deepest reserves. The puppet may fall out of the stage, your object lesson may not work, or the kids may be bored with your presentation. Be ready in your preaching to change direction with the flow of the Spirit or the attention span of the children.

A well-prepared, prayer-soaked message will withstand broken sound equipment, undisciplined bus kids, or parents' interruptions. Check your message this week. Have the children of your church been drinking from the well or has it been an occasional sip from a rusty bucket? Pray for God's anointing and His best each time you step into the preaching portion of your children's church.

The preached Word of God will change lives, bring healing, and free boys and girls who are in the bondage of this world. Let all that you do lead to a time of response.

Look to God for the message, then for the best method.

7

★ ★

BEYOND A LITTLE TALK WITH JESUS

Children are wonderful when it comes to prayer. They pray for dogs and cats and television personalities and stuffed ducks. You tell a child that God wants us to pray, and he will do it. But where does a child learn how to pray?

In the home, prayer or lack of it is taught at the dinner table and bedside. It is experienced in the knocks and victories of everyday living. A wise parent does not relegate prayer to a twice-a-day-only-when-we-have-to kind of activity. Prayer can and should be woven in to every part of a child's living.

This is a day of broken and blended families. Prayer does not always receive the emphasis it deserves in the home. It is important to give prayer a place of prominence in the children's church. You have opened the service with prayer, prayed for special needs, and prayed over the offering. Before the children even arrived in the room, you prayed for a message from God and an anointing on the delivery of that message. You pray with your staff and with children who will minister in this week's service.

TEACH US TO PRAY

When the disciples approached Jesus concerning prayer, He did not turn away. They said, "Lord, teach us to pray." Jesus then set a pattern with what we call the Lord's Prayer.

Like the disciples of old, children desire a pattern. I believe children are looking to you and me for instruction in this area. Again they are crying, "Teach us to pray!" Paul exhorted the church to "pray without ceasing." Tell that to a seven-year-old and he will reply, "How?"

Your example, attitude, and love of prayer will become important instructional tools. Frequency of prayer is limited only by the depth of your love and continuing relationship with Jesus. Children learn by your life that prayer is not just a tool of acquisition, but a time of acquaintance with your first love, Jesus. Prayer must appear important to you if it is to gain importance in the lives of the children you serve. We know that fabulous things can and do happen when people pray in faith believing.

Once in our children's church in Minnesota, a need was brought to our attention. A little girl told me in a worried voice about the son of a man who worked with her dad: The boy was hurt in a sledding accident. She could not tell us his name but she knew that he was in critical condition. I stood a child in the middle of the room, laid hands on him, and prayed for the nameless boy. After prayer time our service continued.

I found the boy and his mother at the hospital on Tuesday morning. She told me that on Saturday evening doctors had instructed her and her husband to begin funeral arrangements. The boy had multiple internal injuries, some of which had destroyed vital organs. She reported that on Sunday morning, at exactly the time we had prayed, her son had been healed. The boy pulled out the plugs and asked his mother for something to eat.

I can't explain the healing power of Jesus. I only know that He inspired the writer to say, "Cast your cares on Him for He cares for you." Jesus does care for every boy and girl in every family.

He is a personal, loving Savior who desires the best for His children. When Jesus physically walked this earth, He took children in His arms and touched and blessed them. I believe He is still touching and blessing the lives of boys and girls today. So allow for that opportunity.

A Time for Response

Make everything you pray and say and demonstrate in the children's church service point to a time of decision. Your entire service should culminate in a designated time of response. If you wish, call it an altar call. This time of prayer is singularly important and should not be forgotten or rushed.

This scenario has happened in almost every children's church (there are variations, but the pattern is constant): You encourage the children to bow their heads in prayer. In your most serious tone, you invite response to the day's message. Some children raise their hands or come forward for prayer. Soft music is playing and the presence of God is real.

Suddenly the back door bursts open and Mrs. Fluster dashes into the room. Bless God, church was good but now it's over. Pastor began his altar service and Mrs. Fluster needs to grab little Mary and run for the car: "Dinner is going to burn and it's Super Bowl Sunday. Papa Fluster is out revving up the Chevy, so grab your Bible and run!" Her hurry is evident as she trips over chairs looking for little Mary. The wonderful girl is praying at the far side of the altar. Her mother grabs her and drags her from the room. Your prayer time is destroyed. Any work God had begun is now terminated.

Scenario two is the quick prayer and run. In the middle of your illustrated sermon, an usher steps through the back door, signaling that church is out. Parents begin peeking their heads in and you know you had better end the service. You close in a quick prayer and the children leave. Again your children's church has ended in frustration.

I have discovered a couple of little tricks for doing away with these kinds of frustrations. You can close and lock your back doors. Place a large sign in bold print on the door saying something like, "Work of God in progress. Do not interrupt the work of the Holy Spirit. Please wait outside until children are dismissed." One children's church leader painted a sign that read, "Do not enter. Negatives being exposed to the Light."

Of course you can always place a former pro-wrestler at the door to help parents wait. Chances are, this kind of approach will be met with some disbelief or even animosity of the parents. We do, from time to time, place a polite assistant at the door to calmly keep the parents from entering during prayer.

However, the early altar call seems to be the easiest solution to disrupted prayer. Time has been set aside to allow children plenty of opportunity for prayer. Here is how to plan for adequate prayer time.

Check the average estimated time of departure. At our church, the morning adult service is usually over by 12:15. That is our estimated time of departure. Back up from this time, fifteen to twenty minutes. This is your designated altar service time. In my case, the prayer time is set at 11:55 each week. This gives us plenty of time to pray without adult interruptions. I have had weeks when the children took all of that time and more. Then again, there

A former pro-wrestler can help deter interrupting parents.

are times when they pray for two or three minutes and then stare at me. When this happens we play Bible quiz games or present a reinforcing object lesson.

Each Sunday one of my helpers is assigned the duty of having a lesson ready for postprayer emergency. Then, if allotted prayer time is not used up, we are not caught flat-footed. Bible quiz games can always reinforce what we have learned that day.

Now you ask the question, "What do you do in the prayer (altar) time?" As with the rest of the service, I want the children to be active participants in prayer. Never allow prayer to become a boring exercise. Use different methodology from week to week.

While the prayer time is underway I always play mellow praise music in the background. I have listed, with explanation, several methods we employ in order to keep prayer time interesting.

ALTAR CALL

This is the Billy Graham-type approach. The theme for the day is emphasized and children are encouraged to respond individually. A child wishing to respond raises his hand and is asked to stand and walk to the front of the room. Upon arrival at the altar he is met by a helper who prays with him. From time to time, a prayer is recited and repeated by those responding. At the conclusion of any prayer time, children are escorted back to their seats.

ALTAR SERVICE

In this prayer time, all children are asked to stand. We gather them all about the altar at the front of the room and together we pray and sing worship songs. These have been some of the most precious prayer times I have experienced.

PRAYER AT THE CHAIR

The children are asked to kneel at their seats and pray. Those with special needs or wanting a prayer partner are told to raise a hand. My workers and I circulate around the room praying for special needs. When a child is done praying he can quietly sit in his chair or sing along with whatever praise music is playing.

SMALL GROUPS

From the front of the room I divide the boys and girls into groups of four or five. This is not a matter of their choice: I assign each child to a group, with whom he will pray. I then direct the groups to various corners of the room, where they are led in prayer by one of my helpers.

PRAYER PARTNERS

Divide the kids into groups of two. The two exchange names and phone numbers and pray for each other during your altar time. Then they call each other on the phone throughout the week and share in prayer.

CIRCLE PRAYING

If your group is small enough or you have a large room, stand in a circle holding hands. Pray around the circle, each child making his or her requests known out loud. A child not wanting to speak out loud may simply say, "unspoken," or squeeze the hand of the next child, signaling him to pray. The leader can close in prayer, mentioning both the spoken and unspoken needs.

Pray for creativity in your prayer service. Give adequate time for this most important portion in the balance of your children's church. An imbalance in this area will send children home with no practical application to the message. Please do not plan a wonderful lesson and leave them wondering how it applies to their lives.

Time spent in prayer is always worthwhile and will many times lead to life-altering decisions. God can do much to change even the most unruly child during a serious moment of prayer.

As one friend of mine said, "Why spend all that time in preparing and presenting a message and close with no time of response?" Give children the privilege of being touched by God. Give them a weekly time of prayer and commitment of themselves to Him. Promotion day will come and the kids will begin to attend the adult service. Your pastor will be blessed to see an honest open response in these who have learned that prayer is an important part of every service.

At the conclusion of the response prayer time, I typically give the kids two or three ideas for immediate application of the lesson. This may take the form of helping mom without complaining or showing mercy to a younger brother. After this, we close our service with prayer.

Prayer is a vital part of every valid worship service. Evaluate your prayer time. Make time for this exercise of Christian life.

8

★ ★

MAKING PARENTS A PART OF THE CHILDREN'S CHURCH EXPERIENCE

You have just experienced a fantastic service. At the conclusion parents are stopping by to take their children home. Suddenly some well-meaning mom steps from the crowd and, wringing your hand, says, "Thank you so much for watching our kids. I don't know what we would do on Sunday mornings without you."

She thinks you are babysitting. Of all the nerve! What is the matter with her?

The matter is that you have never trained this woman or the other parents. She doesn't know you are having church. How will parents ever know you are having a service if you do not allow them to visit once in a while?

Remember, the biblical pattern has always been that parents take the lead in teaching spiritual concepts to their children. Scripture is packed with exhortations to Mom and Dad concerning this mandate. Parents are compelled to teach their children about God.

"Parents, instruct your children in the Word of God. Do this while you are walking down the road, watching television, out for pizza, sitting around the dinner table, shooting hoops, or preparing for bed.

"Do this so that they will know and love Jesus every

day. Do this so that their Christianity will have meaning every hour. Do this so that they will grow up and teach their children of the love of Jesus" (Deuteronomy 6:7–9, Gruber paraphrase).

Parents must take an active part in the child's church experience. This is not only biblical, but it gives you extra helpers on Sunday morning.

Now you are going to ask, "How can I get parents out of the adult service and into the real world?" Adults love to worship God without the interference of children. Kids love to worship God without the interference of parents. So how are you going to merge the two?

The task is not easy. You must commit yourself to a campaign of education that will encompass every church publication. This noble crusade will impose upon your personal time, in phone calls and visitation. It will eat away at your office hours and tax your administrative competence.

Do all you can to inform the parents. Send home a note each month notifying them of the theme and re-inforcing Scripture that will be used in your children's church. You may want to include ideas for carrying the theme into family life and devotions.

Use every church mailer and bulletin to carry testimonies of the goodness of God in your children's church. The printed word will get through to some of the parents.

Every time you see the pastor, give him a short praise report regarding your service. Many times he hears from you only when your ministry has a financial need. Condition him to believe that there is something spiritual happening in your children's church. (Be honest, of course.)

Set a goal of visiting each child's home. This is great for building rapport with the child as well as with the parent. In your visit share the beauty of the children in worship, the wonder of their ministry in the giving time, the joy of preaching to them, and the power of your altar times. However, do not recruit in your visit to the home. Let the home be a sanctuary from high-pressure sales. Once you get to know the parent it is much easier to ask for help when needs arise.

We have "Meet the Saint" scheduled as a regular feature in our children's church. This is a time when the children can meet a parent or other church member. The saint is asked to visit the service on a specified Sunday. He will not have to prepare a lesson or preach to the children.

The only requirements for this are (1) that the person is a Christian, (2) that he be living for Jesus, (3) that he arrive before children's church begins, and (4) that he stay until "Meet the Saint" time.

You guessed it! "Meet the Saint" time is usually held at the end of the service. I want that saint to experience the entire children's church service. I want him to see that we are *not* babysitting; we are *not* having a circus.

The "Meet the Saint" guest-initiate is invited to come to the front of the room. The children's church leader interviews him. I want the kids to know that a housewife or insurance agent or carpenter or trash collector can live for Jesus. Interview the person and leave a short time for questions from the kids. At the end of this time, thank the saint and encourage the kids to greet and talk to him whenever they see him in church or in the community.

We have had a variety of people in for "Meet the Saint." The most memorable among them include a soldier and a church board member.

The soldier was a marine sergeant. He came in full battle fatigues and spoke of being both a Christian and a soldier. It was a fabulous testimony. Many of our boys found a real-life GI Joe for a hero.

The board member came and shared his occupation. He then told about the duties of a deacon and spent time praying for every child. It was a very touching moment in our service as he laid hands on children and prayed. (When your board members experience the service, you no longer have trouble with requests for equipment.)

Another way to get parents through the door is to set up a schedule requiring their attendance. Parents can sign up or submit to the draft. Do not put them up front as a minister but rather in the seats with the kids as a participant. Allow them to join the congregation in worship, giving, preaching, and prayer.

Parents should participate as much as possible in every outing, field trip, or party you throw for the children. Moms and dads need this kind of ministry experience. A wise administrator will seek a one to four parent-child ratio at such events. Parental involvement or lack of it can make or break these types of events.

You will want to include parents in any and every service and activity you can. This comes by prayer, fasting, phone calls, and personal notes. It can be a long and difficult process, but the parents will begin to catch your vision. Without a vision, the children's church will perish.

Begin right now to think of the parents as friends. Build friendships with them and discover a truth I learned long ago: It is hard to quit a friend. Pray for wisdom in this. Enjoy the beauty of it as God faithfully assists you in strengthening families through the children's church.

One last note: Be sensitive to the single parents. Many of the children you minister to are from single parent or blended family homes. (Make special allowance in your attendance contests for the child who is there only twice a month. He has no control over the parent who fails to bring him to children's church.)

When you hold special parent-child events, arrange for adopt-a-parent as the need arises. Take time to listen to, comfort, and provide spiritual and physical assistance

"Meet the Saint" lets children meet church members.

for these families.

I am from a family that was broken by divorce. It was not an easy situation, but God in his rich mercy worked through a few faithful saints to supply help when needed.

Be open to what God would have you do with the parents of your church. If you stay there long enough, you will witness today's children becoming tomorrow's parents. The parents of today will be grandpas and grandmas. You will be blessed as you minister to the next generation side by side with these concerned Christian models.

Share your vision; involve the parents. I know you are not a babysitter and you know you are not a babysitter, but you want them to know too.

9

★ ★

SMORGASBORD

This chapter is devoted to all of the little things I wanted to say to you. Most of the items fall into the category of practical advice. I feel they will be of interest and help to you. So look upon this as a kind of smorgasbord.

CREATIVITY

So many times I have been approached by teachers and leaders of children who have said, "I am not a creative person. I can't tie balloons or sing or draw chalk pictures." Perhaps you sit there thinking similar thoughts right now.

Forget it! You are creative. You have been created in the image of God. His Holy Spirit dwells in the heart of every believer. The creative force of the universe, Jesus Christ, has taken abode in your life. You are creative.

Do not mistake methodology for creativity. Any person can attend seminars and schools to learn visual methods. The average uncoordinated person can learn how to juggle, use puppets, and even trace a picture onto a sheet of butcher's paper. This does not, however, involve the creativity level of that individual.

One dictionary says *create* means "to produce through

imaginative skill." It is the act of bringing into existence something new. This creativity is part of your ministry arsenal. Expertise in several methods will increase this arsenal. You will have greater ease in capturing the attention of the kids as you use your creativity.

Perhaps your imagination has been idling for some time. Give it a tune-up and begin to create. Use creativity in your everyday life. Step beyond the mediocre norms in your approach to problem solving and simple survival. Cultivate this God-infused creativity.

Open your eyes and see the excitement of living in this colorful world. Study God's creativity through the good earth around you. It is amazing what God has created. Look in the mirror. Smile a while and give your face a rest.

When I am not feeling very creative, I do one of two things. First, I spend time observing my children at play. Children have not yet unlearned creativity. Their play is, without reservation, filled with imagination. Simple blocks become airplanes or animals. Anything with wheels can drive through large cities, cultivate fields of crops, or explore jungle paths.

If watching my children doesn't inspire me, I view an hour or two of public television, go to a toy store, or build on to my house.

Above all, be yourself. If God had wanted Dick Gruber to teach in your children's service each week, He wouldn't have placed you there. You are God's perfect choice for those kids at this time. Be creative in your presentation and the children will gladly respond to the message.

ENVIRONMENT

Step into your children's church room. Place a paper sack on your head and listen. Listen to the sounds of the room. What noises are entering from the great beyond?

Children want a room suitable for kids, not giants.

Now take the sack off and kneel down. From that vantage point, look around, observe the room. Is it colorful? Is it boring?

While on your knees you begin to see the room as the children do. Viewing it from the child's eye level you may notice that chalkboards are too high on the wall or visuals are not easily seen from the back row.

Now while still on your knees, pray. Pray that God will help you to make this room more visually appealing.

Move to a chair. Is it the right size for little boys and girls? Scrunch down in the chair. Now your eyes are at the level of the child who sits there. Can he see your face, puppets, other visuals? Will his view cause him to squirm and move and disrupt your worship?

Basically I am telling you to think like a child. Children

do not want to enter a room made for giants. They want to sit in a chair the right size and still be able to see the lesson being presented.

Smell your room. Does it need a good airing out? Buy some air freshener (not the kind that smells like a hospital).

If your room is cluttered and musty and drab, you cannot hope to hold the child's attention. Environment can cause discipline frustrations for even the best of teachers. Take care of your classroom and it will become a help instead of a hindrance to your ministry.

By the way, clean up after yourselves. If the kids trash the place during game show Sunday, then bless them with the thrill of cleaning it up. Teach them to be good stewards of church properties in this way.

DISCIPLINE

I believe in discipline. A well-ordered children's church service is healthy for the spiritual formation of children. But there is a difference between discipline and punishment.

Punishment is a temporary answer to an eternal problem. Discipline holds an eternal answer. Punishment focuses on getting even. Discipline helps a child build a positive self-image and grow in self-control.

Punishment says, "If you do that one more time, I am going to send you to the adult service to sit by your parents." You have just taught the child that it is punishment to sit in church by his parents, that it is punishment to listen to the pastor preach. So when he is promoted out of your department and the doors to the children's church are closed to him, it is unlikely that he will become enthusiastically involved in the adult church.

Children want discipline and loathe punishment.

I once heard in a workshop that discipline is needed and includes instruction, correction, and encouragement.

Now isn't that N.I.C.E.? Children do need and want discipline. The discipline they are taught in church will spill over into every area of life. The Christian life is one of discipline. After all, self-discipline is a fruit of the Spirit.

★ ★

DISCIPLINE IS... Needed
Instruction
Correction
Encouragement

★ ★

Instruct the child in patient love. Let's have no finger-wagging, nagging teachers in children's church. Let him know what was done wrong and why it is important. Show the benefits of obedience as outlined in Scripture. Take this opportunity to train him up in the way he should go.

Correction is a process which turns the offender from bad to good. This may include a stiff lecture but always is laced with and includes prayer. Pray with the child and allow him to pray. Repentance is the act of turning from evil to do right.

Encouragement recognizes the worth of the child in your sight and God's. Let him know that you believe he can follow your rules. Encourage him to be a doer of the Word of God, not a hearer only.

Now here are some thoughts about discipline to keep in mind.

Before you have a disruption:
1. Decide never to use corporal punishment. Children must never be physically assaulted by anyone at church. Spanking, rough-housing, slapping, or dragging have no place in your children's church.
2. Develop and reinforce simple rules. This lets them know your expectations and gives you a base for discussion when discipline becomes necessary.
3. Remind them of your rules. Each Sunday you will want to begin your service with a reminder of your rules for church time. From time to time, without great fanfare, restate the rules. Repetition is the key to learning.
4. Never brag on the consequences of disobedience. The minute you tell them what will happen if they break your rules, some boy will do it just to see if you are serious.
5. Be positive. I tell the kids each week that they can obey the rules. Proverbs 16:21 says, "Pleasant words promote instruction." Be pleasant. Positive messages from the teacher throughout a class session can greatly improve overall behavior. You might say, "I like how Dave is . . .", or "I am glad that Jean is doing such a wonderful job obeying our rules."
6. Determine right now to never embarrass a child in front of his peers. Would Jesus make fun of a child's mistakes? Would he disapprove a child's expression of creativity because it is different from others? Would he mock another for all to enjoy? I think not. Treat children with the same respect you desire from them.
7. Visit the home whenever possible. There is no substitute for a relationship with the child and his parents. A visit to the home will tell you much about the effects of life-style on behavior. You learn much about a child when seeing his room at home. Begin to understand him through his everyday environment.

When disruptive behavior is present:

1. Change your activity. Perhaps you are the problem. If more than a couple of children are getting restless, shift gears and get them actively involved in the message. My mother says, "If the children are busy, they don't have time to be discipline problems." Mom ought to know. She has taught elementary school since I was a class clown in the third grade.

2. Walk in the child's direction. A bit of eye contact and a step or two toward the child will many times cause a cease-fire without a single word uttered.

3. Put your hand on the child's shoulder. Sometimes a hand gently placed on the shoulder will help a child with that temporary lack of self-control.

4. Use the two-week rule. If a child disrupts your class two weeks in a row, then talk to his parents. You may discover a reason for this new behavior. (You may find out the parents are part of the problem.)

5. Pray for the children who become disruptive. Pray that God will surround them with his peace and give you an extra dose of compassion.

6. Provide the shadow. If a child becomes a continuing nuisance, assign an adult worker of the same gender to sit by him and take him out when necessary. This "shadow" continues to teach the child and returns him to the room when peace reigns again.

7. Switch seating. Never return a child to the same seat after you have talked and prayed with him. Seat him somewhere else in the room so that he might not be tempted by his regular audience. He will also be motivated to behave the next time he sits with his friends so that he might remain with them.

Games

I heard it said once or twice that a child's work is his play. Kids love games and learn valuable lessons for living from them.

I do not use games on a weekly basis. In our children's church, games are generally reserved for the postprayer time (if any exists). Games may begin after the final prayers are said. In effect, we close all serious times of meeting with God before we open the Bible Bowl.

These games are designed to reinforce both general and specific Bible knowledge, the latter having been taught during the preceding service.

A great percentage of the time, the games we use pit one half of the room against the other. Boys can compete against the girls, but we make this no requirement.

An effort is made to keep competition on a friendly Christlike level. We wish to have fun. There is no place in the church for highly competitive, Little League kinds of games.

Here are some of the games we use.

Teddy Bear in the Wastebasket

A large trash container is placed on a table or the piano. About six feet away, a tape line is placed on the floor. Another tape line is laid out somewhere in the rear of the room. (This game reflects the fact that I do not like to spend money.) Children answering a lesson-related question may throw a teddy bear from one of the lines. If teddy falls into the basket, points are awarded to the appropriate team. More points are given for a basket from the line farthest from the wastebasket.

Tic-tac-toe

A representative from each team is designated to play the game. Team members answer questions to earn the right for their representative to place his mark on the board. Some people have created magnetic or flannel board versions of this. I use a dry erasable marker board.

Quiz Down

The children are divided into two teams. Each team stands in a single-file line at the front of the room. One by one they are asked questions. A correct answer allows the child to stay at the front of the line. An incorrect answer will send a child to the back of his line. He should have another opportunity to answer before the game is over.

You may also mark a line with tape on the floor. Every child who answers correctly takes a step over that line. The team having the most players standing over the tape line when the parents arrive wins.

THE RACE

There are a multitude of variations to this game. One is to stand two empty soda-pop bottles on a table. A funnel is placed in the mouth of each of them. For every correct team answer, a predetermined amount of liquid is poured into their bottle. The bottle which is filled first declares a winner.

WACKY OLYMPICS

"Strange" and "wonderful" are the key words for this type of game. One church had kids running to the back of the room, popping a balloon, pushing a toddler toy to the front, and hitting a buzzer pad before they could answer a question. Dream big and use those old toddler toys that are cluttering your closets at home.

MOTIVATION

Einstein once said, "Ninety-eight percent of education is motivation."

I read that once and said to myself, "Hey, myself! This is absolutely true!" Discipline difficulties dissipate whenever I discover what motivates a particular child.

The big question comes immediately to mind: How can I motivate the kids so that they will want to participate in the children's church service? What is it that motivates children?

Before we jump off the deep end, before we tackle the tacky, before we dig into the world's largest banana split or give away the three-foot chocolate Easter rabbit—let us look at the purpose for motivating children.

I always approach motivation from an individual stand-point. A teacher once told me, "We don't teach lessons, we teach individuals." Every child is motivated differently.

Educators often talk about intrinsic and extrinsic motivation. Intrinsic refers to motivation from within. Extrinsic is from without.

The intrinsically motivated child has an enthusiastic desire to achieve. This personal momentum comes from within. He is a self-starter. He is a "gifted" student. This child needs no push from the teacher. He will memorize the Scripture, teach the story, and even volunteer for prayer.

A smart teacher will recognize the intrinsically motivated child and simply point him in the right direction. My daughter Sarah is one of these. When assigned a project of any kind, Sarah desires to accomplish it as quickly and with as much perfection as possible. Mom and Dad do not have to push, plead, or threaten. This is reflected in her scholastic achievement.

When it comes to household chores, however, this same wonderfully self-motivated daughter needs an extrinsic push. This brings an important point to mind. A child, or adult, can be extrinsically or intrinsically motivated at different times and for different reasons.

Extrinsic motivation is that power from the outside. It is the child that pushes the lawn mower; the mower wouldn't move without being pushed. And the child wouldn't push without the parents' threats of bodily harm or promise of allowance. And the parents wouldn't threaten and give money if they were not afraid of the neighbors' opinion. Everyone is motivated externally in this scenario.

In the children's church, extrinsic motivation takes on the guise of prizes. Star charts, candy bars, and free trips to local restaurants or amusement parks all serve as external motivations.

Even the serious, service-seeking children's pastor will have an occasional contest or big day. Contests can help bring in more children and control the ones you have. The key is not to let the contests control you.

My goal, however, is always to move children from the external to the internal to the *eternal*.

A child may memorize a Scripture in order to win a prize. Once that Scripture finds its way from the child's head to his heart, a desire to learn more is planted. This child then learns Scripture even when there is no prize offered. Eventually he will apply those verses eternally as he gives his life to Jesus.

A girl at a kids crusade once brought twenty-seven visitors. She bribed her friends with promises of puppets, prizes, and ice cream cones on the way home. The friends came and found a warm, fun place. They were internally motivated to return night after night. Some of those friends found Jesus in that crusade. They had moved from the external to the internal to the eternal.

The girl after winning the visitor contest said, "I started bringing kids 'cause I wanted the big prize. Then I saw some of the kids at the altar and just wanted to bring more."

Boys and girls are motivated by so many different things. Take time to discover what motivates the children you serve. Apply this knowledge as you plan future services.

10

★ ★

FAMILY WORSHIP: CHILDREN SHOULD BE SEEN *AND* HEARD

I have stated earlier that one of the purposes of a children's church is to prepare children for a meaningful transition into adult worship. Is children's church in a balanced service format enough? I hardly think so. Children need parental reinforcement and regular visits to the adult or family worship setting.

"Little children were brought to Jesus for him to place his hands on them and pray for them. But the disciples rebuked those who brought them. Jesus said, 'Let the little children come to me, and do not hinder them, for the kingdom of heaven belongs to such as these'" (Matthew 19:13–14).

In many churches today, children are given no opportunity to worship, give, or respond to the pastor's preaching. The common practice which is sweeping our nation is *parallel child care*. What I mean by this is that every time the doors of the church are opened for service, child care (children's service or circus time) is provided.

We are, in practice, raising a generation of potential church dropouts. These children have never experienced a multi-generational worship service. They have not had opportunity to become enculturated to the adult worship mode. In my denomination alone an alarming rate of almost 37 percent of these children will filter out of our back doors in their 7th and 8th grade years.

Yet pastors will stand and declare the success of the Sunday evening service. I heard one pastor excitedly proclaim. "We just couldn't get people out on Sunday nights until we started a Sunday evening children's church. Now we have the biggest crowds ever."

Perhaps it is a societal trend. Adults are looking for a country club church experience: Pay their dues, claim their pews, and hear the news. Like the country club, the church hires others to take care of unwanted duties such as child care, maintenance, and cooperative service. In the country club you can attend when you feel like it, without obligation.

Let me challenge you to break from the Matthew 19:13 kind of church agenda. Refuse to accept the mistaken notion that the children would be better served somewhere out of sight and sound of their parents. This practice serves the adult adherents with no regard to the long-term effect on the spiritual development of the child.

Children need family worship. Parents need family worship. Scripture indicates God's desire to include children in worship and instruction:

"There was not a word of all that Moses had commanded that Joshua did not read to the whole assembly of Israel, including the women and children, and the aliens who lived among them" (Joshua 8:35).

"All the men of Judah, with their wives and children and little ones, stood there before the Lord" (2 Chronicles 20:13).

"And on that day they offered great sacrifices, rejoicing because God had given them great joy. The women and children also rejoiced. The sound of rejoicing in Jerusalem could be heard far away" (Nehemiah 12:43).

"But when the chief priests and the teachers of the law saw the wonderful things he did and the children shouting in the temple area, 'Hosanna to the Son of David,' they were indignant. 'Do you hear what these children are saying?' they asked him. 'Yes,' replied Jesus, 'have you never read, "From the lips of children and infants you have ordained praise"?'" (Matthew 21:15–16).

It is our task as church leaders to educate our constituency. Therefore, I urge you:

★ Allow children to worship. Children want to worship God. They want to worship by Mom and Dad's side. Children need to witness the faithfulness of their parents as they give tithes and offerings, take notes on the pastor's sermon, and respond at the altar.

★ Accommodate children in worship. Give children a place in your total church worship goals. The reason many children do not participate in so-called family worship services is that such services have not been designed for the entire family. They are simply adult services with children present. When children are not given a part in these services, parents become frustrated disciplinarians instead of intent worshipers.

★ Assist children in worship. All ages should be encouraged to worship. Helps can be provided that will make children feel a part of your family service. God does inhabit the praises of His people. Point out that there is no age limit on worship set in Scripture, that everybody in the body of Christ should be included.

Thomas Trask, wrote, "Worship is the act of giving honor, respect, and reverence to a Being who is worthy of the same. So real worship ought to mean continual conversion of thoughts, standards, and aims from a self-centered to a God-centered focus" (*And He Gave Pastors: Pastoral Theology in Action*, Thomas F. Zimmerman, ed., [Springfield, Mo.: Gospel Publishing House, 1979], 282.)

Our aim in children's ministry is to assist children in this conversion. We, through our example, our relationships with God and the student, and our inclusion of children in a variety of worship experiences, can see this life-style emerge. Children need family worship experiences as much as they need children's church.

A child typically attends Sunday school and children's church on Sunday mornings. He is being trained in the way he should go. In Sunday school, doctrine is systematically presented using a variety of methods. In children's church, the gospel is presented in a worship format. Children give praise to God, learn and respond to a message, and participate up front. This is all geared to a child's level of understanding and provides peer reinforcement for positive spiritual growth.

As I have already said, our task is one of preparing children for sixty or seventy years of participation in adult worship. The kind of worship Thomas Trask writes about needs more than can be provided in the children's church setting. The family worship service completes the cycle of training that a child needs for healthy and continued involvement in corporate worship.

MAKING SERVICES CHILD-FRIENDLY

Your efforts to make this time child-friendly will strongly carry the message to parents that your church loves families. But remember these points in doing this:

⭐ Don't do the same thing every week. For example, using even the most exciting puppets can become mundane and boring when overused.

⭐ Do not talk down when addressing the children. Those in positions of authority in the family worship should treat children as part of the Body. A voice may be softened without sounding phony or singsongy. If pastors and other church leaders treat children with respect, it will be mirrored in the children's attitudes toward them.

★ Involve children whenever and however you can. There is no surer way to interest the body of young believers than to place one of their friends in the limelight. (The children will sit up and take notice if only to watch their friend make a mistake.)

★ Don't worry about perfection. Children will not do a perfect job every time they are up front. The wonder is that your congregation will overlook imperfection on a child's part. Parents and non-parents alike will sit on the edge of their seats rooting for a child. You can't go wrong when allowing a child to minister up front. People will enjoy it and the child who has had the opportunity will grow up with a leaning toward ministry.

Here are some ways to develop a truly family worship service, accommodating the children.

Prayer

★ Boys and girls want to pray. It takes only a word of encouragement from the pulpit to include them. Many times they sit back and watch because the prayer time is perceived as an adult event. An invitation should be given verbally to the children. If they don't hear you say "boys and girls," chances are they will believe you are not speaking to them.

★ When asking for prayer requests, include the children. Some churches keep a stack of prayer request cards in each pew. Children and adults are encouraged to fill them out and drop them in the offering bag as it passes. Treat every request sincerely. By doing so, you are training children in the importance of prayer. You will also, through this action, instill in children the reality of the verse, "Cast all your anxiety on him because he cares for you" (1 Peter 5:7).

⭐ Encourage families to sit together and hold hands to pray. Part of our mission on earth is to strengthen the family. A bond of prayer is not easily broken.

⭐ A child can be invited to offer prayer during any part of the service: upon its opening, during prayer request time (including prayer for the sick), for the offering, or at the service's conclusion.

⭐ Children are marvelous prayer warriors. When inviting people down for prayer, ask if any children would like to pray for others. You will be surprised at the number of children who take this ministry seriously. Children come to Jesus with simple faith and great things happen.

SPECIAL SERVICES

⭐ At least once a month your church should present missions. A short lesson or story will interest the children and serve to place importance on missions.

⭐ Include children in the planning of special church days. For instance, children can participate in annual Christmas or Easter programs. They can play a big part in helping with the Sunday night kick-off of a kids crusade or vacation Bible school.

⭐ Many churches hold an occasional service run by the youth group. Teens lead in prayer, worship, receive the offering, and preach. Why not bring this down a step? With the supervisory assistance of Sunday school teachers, children can lead a service for your congregation several times a year.

SERMONS

✪ When I preach in an evening family service, I begin by giving the main points of my sermon. I then ask the children if they will help me remember these points. We repeat the points together, and as the sermon progresses I depend on the children to shout out the points from time to time so that we all remember where the sermon is headed and when it will be over.

✪ Keep sermons in the family worship service short and to the point. Good meat doesn't have to be surrounded by excessive entrees. Use storytelling skills to your advantage. Children and adults love to hear a good story.

✪ Illustrate the sermon whenever possible. Jesus used object lessons and other illustrative means to drive home deep spiritual thoughts. Your congregation will not only enjoy illustrated sermons, but they will retain and live the message that has been preached.

✪ Many pastors take a segment of the Sunday service to invite children up front for a talk. This little chat with the pastor helps children grow in love and appreciation for their pastor. A pastor who gives time to the children can expect reasonable attention from them at other times in the service.

✪ Perhaps the most radical concept is to allow children to actually preach or teach before the congregation. There are children that have a gift of teaching. These boys and girls love to share Bible knowledge with others. A child may explain one point of the sermon or give the whole sermon.

MUSIC AND WORSHIP

✪ Invite some children to join your worship team. Many churches have a team of three or four adults who lead in congregational worship. Including children on this team will immediately gain the attention of all children present.

⭐ Many children take instrumental music lessons through either private teachers or public schools. The public schools will showcase these children in monthly PTA meetings and at local shopping malls. The church, too, should make a place for these kids. Schedule children who have played an instrument a year or longer. When they play in your evening service, younger children will be encouraged to begin study and to use this talent for the Lord.

DRAMA

⭐ Puppets can present songs or skits. Adults as well as children enjoy puppet presentations. Puppets can bring a humorous angle to a message that may not be received in any other form of delivery.

⭐ Once in a while a dramatic skit can serve to emphasize a spiritual truth. Allow children to take part in a drama troupe at your church. The whole family will enjoy skits of either a comedic or dramatic nature.

SCRIPTURES

⭐ Invite a child to the pulpit to read the Scripture text for the evening's sermon. Many children have very good reading skills and would gladly participate in this way.

⭐ A pastor I know opens his service each week with prayer. After prayer, he invites anyone, young or old, to share a meaningful verse of Scripture. Many children come ready to quote or read a passage to the entire congregation. This seems to be a fulfillment of 1 Corinthians 14:26 where it says, "What then shall we say, brothers? When you come together, everyone has a hymn, or a word of instruction, a revelation, a tongue or an interpretation. All of these must

Sunday service chats foster love and appreciation for pastors.

be done for the strengthening of the church."

⭐ A demonstration of Scripture knowledge can be presented by children in the evening service. Some pastors are taking a brief time during the service to ask children questions from the Bible. These little quiz times encourage all members present to sharpen their Bible knowledge.

OBJECT LESSONS

⭐ An object lesson can be used to introduce the theme of the evening's sermon. This can be presented by the pastor, a Sunday school teacher, or an older child.

⭐ When using object lessons in your sermon, invite a child or children up front to hold the objects. You can hold an object up yourself, but involving a child will capture the attention of all children present.

OTHER IDEAS

⭐ Print a bulletin just for kids. It can include Bible quiz questions, puzzles, memory verses, word from the pastor, announcements, an outline of the sermon, and a place to take notes or draw pictures.

⭐ Children can, under the direction of the regular ushers, serve in ushering. However, don't do this more than one Sunday a month; you want this kind of ministry to be a special opportunity.

⭐ Give parents a list of questions to be discussed with their children after church. This will encourage both parents and children to pay more attention to what is being said from the pulpit.

⭐ Churches with club ministries should encourage boys and girls to dress in uniform when helping in the evening service. There is no better way to promote an awareness in the congregation of the value of such programs. Seeing happy children in uniform serving God will make a lasting impression on people.

⭐ Most pastors do not like to read announcements. Allow children to take part in announcement time. Have two or three children read them, add your seal of approval, and everybody will pay attention.

⭐ Children can help operate equipment, the most common example being the overhead projector. A child can turn it on and change transparencies as required. In one church I noticed children in the sound booth. The church sound man was training children so that they could run sound for their morning children's church service.

I trust that you will begin to make your Sunday evening service a true family service. You will notice a difference in your congregation. Large or small, a church that includes all ages in a family service will begin to develop a family-friendly feeling, which will reach beyond your walls.

Children and parents will begin to enjoy worship together. As this happens, families will be stronger, response will be heartfelt, and a foundation will be laid for a future of God-centered believers who worship in spirit and in truth.

ALTERNATE PLANS TO THE FAMILY SERVICE

"But what if my senior pastor insists on my running an evening children's program?"

You are a servant. At this juncture you can leave town

or discover creative ways to make this evening program different from your morning Sunday school and church service. Here are a few suggestions:

⭐ Provide a kids' music time. This time can be spent in choir, age-level training, or even group instrumental or voice lessons.

⭐ Some churches use Sunday evening as a time of in-depth doctrinal study. Each denomination has its own course of study for such classes.

⭐ This is an ideal time to involve children in a Bible quiz program. Study, games, and quiz matches can fill this time with something worthwhile.

⭐ Create a junior college of ministry training. Children can be trained in puppetry, clowning, prayer, drama, mime, and even equipment operation. Children who attend can be used in their ministries in the morning children's church, during Sunday school, or once a month in a special evening service for the whole family.

⭐ Many slip into the mode of running a regular children's service. If you do this, be sure to develop segments and characters that differ from your morning service. Variety is the spice of life.

⭐ Learning centers, games, crafts, and other reinforcing activities keep children moving through a time of Bible discovery. Variety and hands-on involvement are the keys to success.

Using one or a combination of these, you can build a quality evening program for children. Do all you can to impress upon leadership the need for corporate inter-generational worship times. If you end up running an evening as well as a morning program for the kids, smile and do your best for Jesus.

11

★ ★

IF I'VE SAID IT ONCE...

Your children's church, is it a circus or a service? Is it a Sunday morning snack session or a banquet table where children taste and see that the Lord is good? Since the day that God placed me in a children's church, I have wanted to be the best I can be. My desire has been to glorify God through every object lesson and puppet spectacular. In every lesson I present, I want the children to be directed to the Cross and the Christ of that Cross.

There have been times of discouragement. There have been times of sorrow and of laughter. There have been times of wonderful blessing and dismal failure.

Through it all, God has kept this desire at the forefront of my mind: *I can always improve what I am doing.* God has always been at my side giving strength and wisdom and creativity. This same marvelous Savior will be at your side.

There is never an excuse for mediocrity in ministry to children. God has placed you in a children's church. That children's church can be a valid worship experience. You can have fabulous props, creative lessons, and powerful altar services.

Go to seminars. Learn all you can about ministry to and through children. Apply those things that will work in your church setting. Adapt or file those things that will not.

But with all the evaluation and sharpening of tools, never forget that God has entrusted you with this task. Your children's church belongs to Jesus. Every week he walks the aisle. He loves the disruptive child. He hugs the lonely child. He desires the worship of every child. He longs for the prayers of each boy and girl.

Remember Jesus in your preparation and presentation. That sounds silly, doesn't it? How could you forget Jesus? This is church. Do like Ezra of old. He "devoted himself to the study and observance of the Law of the Lord, and to teaching its decrees and laws in Israel" (Ezra 7:10).

If you have been entertaining a Sunday morning circus, I pray that the words which you have read will open doors of possibility. You can attain a balance of worship, giving, preaching, and prayer.

Never settle for a circus again. Each week you should strive to prepare children for the fabulous future of adult worship. Each week, your service can be training children for a productive life of servanthood.

And someday when you stand before Jesus, He will say, "I was thirsty and you pushed the button on the water fountain. I was disruptive and you took the time to discipline me. I needed an outlet for my gift of teaching and you allowed me to stand and serve my friends as one of your helpers."

You will say, "Lord, when did I do all of these things?"

And the King will answer, "Whatever you did for and to and with the boys and girls of your children's church, you have done for and to and with me."

What can I say? Quit clowning around and have a service! You will be eternally pleased with the results.

★ ★

OTHER RESOURCES

Cassidy, John, and B. C. Rimbeaux. *Juggling for the Complete Klutz*, 3rd. rev. ed. (includes 3 juggling bean bags). Palo Alto, Calif.: Klutz Press, 1988.

Coleman, William L. *Today I Feel Like a Warm Fuzzy.* Minneapolis: Bethany House Publishers, 1980.

_____. *What Children Need to Know When Their Parents Get Divorced.* Minneapolis: Bethany House Publishers, 1983.

Dresselhaus, Richard. *Teaching for Decision.* Sunday School Staff Training Series. Springfield, Mo.: Gospel Publishing House, 1989.

Eder, Enelle G., and Grace Pulham. *Growing in God's Garden/The Greatest Show on Earth*, 2 Vols. in 1. Springfield, Mo.: Gospel Publishing House, 1989.

Faulkner, Linda. *The Young Christian's Puzzle Book: For Becoming a Grown-Up Christian.* Springfield, Mo.: Gospel Publishing House, 1992.

Higgins, John R. *Meet God! A Young Christian's Handbook for Knowing God.* Springfield, Mo.: Gospel Publishing House, 1988.

Johnson, Douglas W. *The Care and Feeding of Volunteers.* Creative Leadership Series. Nashville: Abingdon, 1978.

Johnson, Laurene, and Georglyn Rosenfeld. Divorced Kids: *What You need to Know to Help Kids Survive a Divorce.* Nashville: Thomas Nelson Publishers, 1990.

Maempa, John. *Foundations for Faith: Introduction to Bible Doctrine* (student kit; teacher's manual). Springfield, Mo.: Gospel Publishing House, 1980.

Marsh, Fredda. *Putting It All Together in a Puppet Ministry.* Springfield, Mo.: Gospel Publishing House, 1978.

Pearson, Mary Rose. *Perky Puppets with a Purpose.* Springfield, Mo.: Gospel Publishing House, 1992.

Zuck, Roy B., Robert E. Clark, and Joanne Brubaker. *Childhood Education in the Church,* rev., exp. ed. Chicago: Moody, 1986.